What's the Issue?

WHAT ARE TAXES?

By Joseph Stanley

KidHaven
PUBLISHING

Published in 2020 by
KidHaven Publishing, an Imprint of Greenhaven Publishing, LLC
353 3rd Avenue
Suite 255
New York, NY 10010

Designer: Andrea Davison-Bartolotta
Editor: Katie Kawa

Photo credits: Cover (top) photofriday/Shutterstock.com; cover (bottom) kenchiro168/ Shutterstock.com; p. 5 (top) SmilingHotei/Shutterstock.com; p. 5 (bottom right) zhu difeng/ Shutterstock.com; p. 5 (bottom middle) Trong Nguyen/Shutterstock.com; p. 5 (bottom left) Rawpixel.com/Shutterstock.com; p. 6 VCG Wilson/Corbis via Getty Images; p. 7 courtesy of the Library of Congress; pp. 9, 21 Number1411/Shutterstock.com; p. 10 courtesy of ourdocuments.gov; p. 11 Alex Wong/Getty Images; pp. 13, 17 Monkey Business Images/Shutterstock.com; p. 15 ESB Professional/Shutterstock.com; p. 16 Joy Prescott/Shutterstock.com; p. 19 (inset) Mark Van Scyoc/ Shutterstock.com; p. 19 (main) Syda Productions/Shutterstock.com.

Library of Congress Cataloging-in-Publication Data

Names: Stanley, Joseph, author.
Title: What are taxes? / Joseph Stanley.
Description: First Edition. | New York : KidHaven Publishing, [2020] |
  Series: What's the issue? | Includes index.
Identifiers: LCCN 2018050622 (print) | LCCN 2018053911 (ebook) | ISBN
  9781534567320 (eBook) | ISBN 9781534530010 (pbk. book) | ISBN
  9781534567313 (library bound book) | ISBN 9781534531246 (6 pack)
Subjects: LCSH: Taxation–United States. | Income tax deductions–United
  States.
Classification: LCC HJ2381 (ebook) | LCC HJ2381 .S723 2020 (print) | DDC
  336.200973–dc23
LC record available at https://lccn.loc.gov/2018050622

Printed in the United States of America

CPSIA compliance information: Batch #BS19KL: For further information contact Greenhaven Publishing LLC, New York, New York at 1-844-317-7404.

Please visit our website, www.greenhavenpublishing.com. For a free color catalog of all our high-quality books, call toll free 1-844-317-7404 or fax 1-844-317-7405.

CONTENTS

Communities Need Money

It costs a lot of money to keep a community running! Fixing roads, paying police officers and firefighters, and building new public schools are just some of the things communities need money to do. Where does this money come from? It comes from taxes.

Taxes are amounts of money paid to local, state, and national governments for services citizens use—from health care to public parks. There are many different kinds of taxes that pay for different services. It's important to know what these taxes are before you need to start paying them.

Facing the Facts 🔍

People have been paying taxes for thousands of years! Citizens of ancient Egypt, Greece, and Rome paid taxes. Before people paid their taxes with money, they often paid the government with crops they grew.

4

Government leaders work hard to make sure tax dollars are used in the best possible way.

Not Very Popular

Paying taxes is an important part of citizenship. Citizens of the United States have rights, and they also have **responsibilities**. Paying taxes is one of their biggest responsibilities.

Although Americans generally understand the importance of taxes, they're sometimes unhappy with how much money they have to pay. In fact, Americans have been **protesting** high taxes for hundreds of years! When what's now the United States was a group of 13 British colonies, high taxes became one of the reasons Americans fought for their freedom in the American Revolution.

Stamp Act stamps

Facing the Facts

In 1765, the Stamp Act was passed by Great Britain to tax printed **materials**, such as newspapers and playing cards, in the American colonies. It was one of the most unpopular taxes in the colonies and was repealed, or officially stopped, the next year.

In 1773, colonists who were angry about the British tax on tea dumped hundreds of chests of tea into Boston Harbor in Massachusetts in protest. This event became known as the Boston Tea Party, and it's an early example of the protests against taxes that continue today in the United States.

Federal, State, and Local Taxes

Taxes continued to play an important part in U.S. history after the colonists became independent. Although they didn't have to pay taxes to Britain anymore, they weren't free from all taxes. The U.S. Constitution, which set up the new U.S. government, gave Congress the power to collect taxes.

Today, Americans continue to pay federal taxes, which are taxes paid to the national government. State and local governments also have the power to collect taxes from citizens. People pay different amounts of money in taxes depending on where in the United States they live.

8

Facing the Facts 🔍

The federal government needs money to run all the branches of the U.S. military and other national security **agencies**. This kind of spending is called defense spending, and it's generally paid for with tax dollars.

These are just some of the things tax dollars are used for in the United States. People often have different opinions about how tax dollars should be spent. What do you think should get the most money from taxpayers?

roads

defense spending

public schools

health care

What do taxes pay for?

bridges

parks

police and fire departments

post offices

The Importance of Income Taxes

Taxes are collected in many different ways. One common kind of tax is an income tax. This is money that's taken out of a person's income, or how much money they earn by working, and given to the government. Most people have money taken out of every paycheck to pay their income tax.

The federal government gets most of its money from this kind of tax. People who make the most money have to pay the most money in federal income taxes. In addition, many states and some local governments also collect income taxes.

Facing the Facts 🔍

In 1913, the 16th **Amendment** to the U.S. Constitution was ratified, or formally approved. This amendment allowed Congress to create a federal income tax.

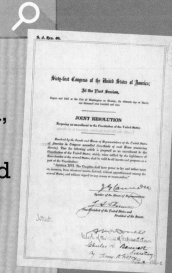

In December 2017, President Donald Trump signed the Tax Cuts and Jobs Act into law. This act changed income taxes in major ways and led to many **debates** about whether those changes would be good or bad for Americans.

11

Funding FICA

Another kind of tax is also taken out of a person's paycheck. It's called a payroll tax or FICA tax. FICA stands for Federal Insurance Contributions Act. This money goes toward two **programs** that help people in the United States.

FICA taxes help pay for Social Security, which is a program that provides money for older people who've stopped working as well as people with disabilities. These taxes also help pay for Medicare. This is a program that provides health care coverage for people over the age of 65 and younger people with disabilities.

Facing the Facts

Around 170 million people in the United States pay FICA taxes every year.

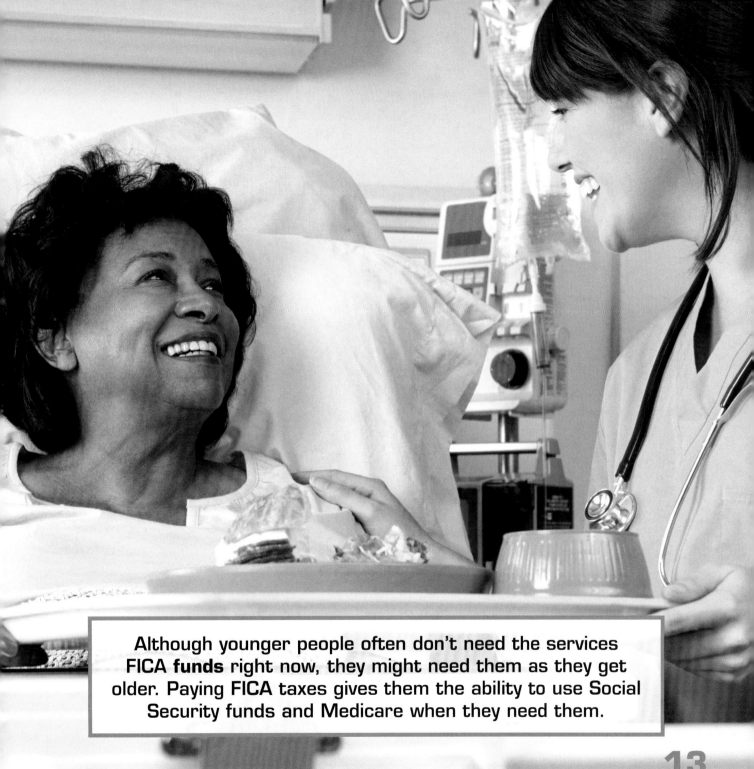

Although younger people often don't need the services FICA **funds** right now, they might need them as they get older. Paying FICA taxes gives them the ability to use Social Security funds and Medicare when they need them.

13

Sales Taxes

Have you ever bought something that ended up costing more money than the price tag showed? In many cases, that extra cost comes from sales taxes. A sales tax is added to the price of goods, and that money then goes to the government.

If you buy things in different places, you might notice that the sales tax isn't always the same. State and local governments can collect their own sales taxes to raise money for things they need. Some states don't make people pay any sales tax.

Facing the Facts

An excise tax is a tax on a **specific** service or good, such as gas for cars. This kind of tax is paid by the business selling the good or service, but they include it in the price **consumers** pay to cover the cost.

The next time you go shopping, check to see if you had to pay a sales tax on what you bought. Now you know what that extra cost is for!

Paying for Property

When people are buying a house, they often ask about the property taxes they'll have to pay. A property tax is a tax on homes, other buildings, and land that a person owns. The local government generally decides how much property tax a person needs to pay based on how much the property is worth.

Because property taxes generally go to local governments, the money goes right into the community a person lives in. Property taxes are used to pay government workers, fix roads, run schools, and do many other important things in a community.

Facing the Facts 🔍

Some places in the United States have no property taxes. For example, in Alaska, only 24 local governments out of 165 are funded by property taxes.

Alaskan homes

Buying a home is a big decision, and property taxes often play an important part in helping people decide what house to buy.

In Trouble with the IRS

Many people don't like paying taxes, but they understand that it's part of their responsibilities as a citizen. Some people, however, try to get away with paying no taxes at all or with paying less than they actually owe. This is called tax evasion, and it's illegal. People can go to jail for not paying their taxes.

The part of the U.S. government in charge of finding cases of tax evasion is the Internal Revenue Service (IRS). The IRS's main job is to collect taxes and to enforce, or make sure people follow, tax laws.

Facing the Facts 🔍

Some people hire accountants to help them with their taxes. An accountant is a person who keeps records of money spent and earned and helps people file their tax returns, which list important tax **information** such as income.

When people pay their taxes, they sometimes worry that they'll get in trouble with the IRS for making a mistake. However, tax evasion can only happen when someone purposely pays too little or none of their taxes.

UNITED STATES

Internal
Revenue
Service
Building

← Visitors
←♿

Sharing Strong Feelings

Many Americans feel very strongly about taxes. They often work hard to earn enough money for themselves and their family, and they don't always like the idea of giving some of that money to the government. They want to know that government leaders are putting their tax dollars to good use.

In some communities, meetings are held about how to spend tax dollars. Citizens can go to these meetings and share their opinions. Everyone has to pay taxes, but everyone also has a right to share their thoughts on what those taxes should be used for.

Facing the Facts

A 2018 study showed that 61 percent of Americans believe the amount of money they're paying in taxes is fair.

WHAT CAN YOU DO?

Learn more about what taxes pay for in your community, state, and country.

Write to government leaders about how you think tax dollars should be used.

Talk to a parent or guardian about the taxes they pay and how they pay them.

Pay attention to the sales tax when you buy things.

If you get an allowance, ask a parent or guardian to take a small amount of money out of it to use for a fun family activity. This helps you practice paying income taxes.

These are some of the things you can do to better understand taxes and to share your educated opinions about taxes with other people. It's never too early to start thinking about this important part of life!

GLOSSARY

agency: A government department that is responsible for a certain activity or area.

amendment: A change in the words or meaning of a law or document, such as a constitution.

consumer: A person who purchased goods or services.

debate: An argument or discussion about an issue, generally between two sides.

fund: To provide money for a special purpose. Also, an amount of money used for a special purpose.

information: Facts about something.

material: Something from which something else can be made.

program: A system under which action may be taken toward a goal.

protest: To speak out strongly against something. Also, an event in which people gather to speak out strongly against something.

responsibility: A duty that a person should do.

specific: Special or particular.

FOR MORE INFORMATION

WEBSITES

Biz Kids: A World Without Taxes

bizkids.com/episode/a-world-without-taxes

The videos on this website help explain taxes to kids, including what community services taxes help fund.

Our Documents: 16th Amendment

www.ourdocuments.gov/doc.php?flash=false&doc=57

This National Archives website features facts about the 16th Amendment, which created the federal income tax, as well as pictures and the text of the document itself.

BOOKS

Barousse, Jason. *The Internal Revenue Service: Why U.S. Citizens Pay Taxes.* New York, NY: PowerKids Press, 2018.

Brennan, Linda Crotta. *Understanding Taxes.* Ann Arbor, MI: Cherry Lake Publishing, 2016.

Steinberg, Lynnae D. *What Are Taxes?* New York, NY: Britannica Educational Publishing, 2016.

INDEX